# THE ESSENCE OF
# BRAZILIAN
# *Jiu-Jitsu*

## By Rigan Machado

## UP

First published in 2002 by
**CFW Enterprises, Inc.**

Copyright © 2002 by
**Unique Publications, Inc.**

**ISBN: 0-86568-194-5**
**Library of Congress Catalog Number: 2001 132414**

Distributed by:
**Unique Publications**
4201 Vanowen Place
Burbank, CA 91505
(800) 332-3330

First edition
05 04 03 02 01 00 99 98 97 1 3 5 7 9 10 8 6 4 2

Printed in the United States of America

Editor: John Steven Soet
Design: George Foon
Cover: George Chen

# Table of Contents

# Acknowledgement

I would like to thank each and every one of my brothers. Additionally, I would like to thank Chuck Norris for his continued support and inspiration, my good friends André Lima, Bill Hoper and Paulo Guillobel.

*— Muito obrigado*

# Dedication

This book is dedicated to my uncle, Carlos Gracie, founder of Brazilian jiu-jitsu.

— *Rigan Machado*

# About the Author

*Carlos Gracie*

Rigan Machado is one of Brazilian grappling's most storied figures. A champion in Brazil, and cousin to the Gracies, Rigan was one of the first black belts to come to the United States and introduce an entire generation to the lost art of ground fighting. In so doing he helped change American martial arts forever. Since then the Machado brothers have appeared on multiple episodes of *Walker: Texas Ranger*, and several Steven Seagal movies. Rigan (along with brothers John, Jean-Jacques, Carlos, and Roger) has become one of most recognizable figures in the world of martial arts. Despite his fame, however, and his many offers to pursue other interests, Rigan continues to train with a dedication born out of the love of his art. In this, his first book, Rigan Machado reveals the intricate techniques of one of the world's most effective fighting systems.

# The Machado Brothers

# Chapter One

# The Science of Submission

With the advent of the no-gi Abu Dhabi Submission Wrestling World Championships, and no-hold-barred events such as the WVC, Pride, Rings, and King of the Cage, the traditional "gi only" training method of Brazilian jiu-jitsu has come under close scrutiny. Rather than defend the method, Rigan has integrated no-gi training methods into the Brazilian jiu-jitsu arsenal. Never one to stay in one place, Rigan Machado is constantly looking for ways to do new things within the framework of the proven Brazilian jiu-jitsu fighting style. As Rigan himself says, "You must adapt the details, but keep the big picture the same. Use all the same tools, just in different ways."

**What is the difference between training with or without the gi?**

The difference is that with the gi, the submission game is much more technical. When you wear the gi, you have many more chances to catch your opponent. You have a chance to use the gi to your advantage. You have much better control for your opening moves. You can tighten up different points on your opponent's body which sets him up for the move to follow. A proper submission, whether it is an arm lock, knee bar, or whatever, is all a result of a proper opening

and that is where the gi is most helpful. When you don't have the gi, you have to use a lot of speed and strength. It is not so much a technical match as it is a physical match — many of the techniques are either limited or completely eliminated. The number of chokes you can attempt are greatly reduced; arm locks are harder to get, because you lose so much leverage that you have to get much closer to your opponent. So there are negatives to not having a gi. However, depending on your strategy, there are also potential advantages to both.

I believe today that it is very important to train both with and without a gi. The way I train is the way I like to teach. I have trained with the gi most of my life. But I like sometimes to challenge myself by adapting the techniques I learned with the gi to grappling without the gi. In this way, I keep myself from getting too comfortable with one way of training — because then you stop learning.

**But don't most top no-holds-barred fighters train exclusively without the gi?**

Yes, that's true I suppose. But in my academy, for example, I have 200 students, but maybe only 10 percent of them want to go into professional fighting. The rest, 90 percent, want to learn jiu-jitsu for fun, for fitness, for self-defense, or to compete in sport tournaments. That's why the sport rules were invented - it's a way to give the students goals for their training. Tournaments are something to shoot for that aren't as violent or intense as professional fighting. And the gi is better for tournaments because it creates more options for the students who are com-

peting in them.

**Do you use different grips when you're using or not using the gi?**

Sure. With the gi, sometimes you can do a lot of different set-ups in order to expose your opponent to a submission. You can keep a comfortable distance from your opponent, stay loose, and still grab the lapel, or the material around the elbow, or even the gi at the hip or the knee, and still control him. But with no gi, the game is much different, you can't control your opponent from a distance and still set him up for a finishing hold. Because a grip that would work with a gi, will be quickly broken without one. There is no lapel to grab, for example, and if you try to hold the neck, the opponent just has to turn his head a little and you slip off. So instead of grabbing for specific points on the body, you have to think about controlling entire regions of the body. For example, instead of controlling the lapel from a distance, you have to get close and control his entire upper body by circling your arms around his body, or by trapping his arm under your arm.

But in either situation, you have to think like a grappler. You have to change your approaches to a move, but you should still be trying to hit the move. In other

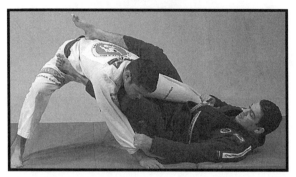

words, don't let the fact that you have or don't have a gi throw you off your grappling strategy — don't let it take you out of your game. Control the situation rather than letting the situation control you. You must adapt the details, but keep the big picture the same. Use all the same tools, just in different ways.

**So chokes are easier to apply with the gi?**

Actually, it really depends on the situation. For example, to do the basic rear naked choke, or the back choke, is much easier without the gi, because your arms get real slippery in a match because of the sweat, and you can slide your arm in much easier and get deeper penetration with less effort. When you have the gi it is sometimes more difficult because the material adds a lot of friction and the arm won't slide in as easily. The gi actually stops the back choke many times. With the gi, when you have the back, I think the collar choke is a much better technique to use. So you have to adapt your entry while keeping the ultimate goal the same: to give your opponent a little nap. It's just with the gi, there are more options.

**So you learn more techniques with the gi?**

There are more techniques because there are more options for each move. For

example, with practicing take-downs, you have a chance to try a judo throw or to use the gi to block when someone tries to sweep you, or to open someone up for you to sweep them. But when you take away the gi, you pretty much take away all the judo throws — or at the very least they are severely limited. It's much easier for you to slip in, go low, and shoot for the legs with a freestyle wrestling technique than it is to try a judo hip throw. So right there you've eliminated the option of the judo throw.

But this is a very relative thing, and it goes both ways depending on what art you've been practicing. When you put a wrestler in a gi, for example, they can easily get lost because they have no idea what to do when someone grabs them by the clothes instead of the body. So a jiu-jitsu man can use that to his advantage. The guard is another example where I use the gi to keep him close to me. Without the gi, a wrestler will have a lot more room to operate. But with the gi I can control him by controlling the gi with my arms, without having to clinch. I can keep him from going to the side more effectively, or in the mount I can keep him from escaping from the bottom. There is much less chance to slip away.

So when I train with the gi, I practice those types of moves that would be to my advantage, and then training without the gi I also focus on those things that will help me the most. However, the key thing to remember is that the angles are always the same. The only thing that changes is the grip — the way you control your opponent for the entry. But everything else is the same.

**Why don't you see a lot of leg locks in jiu-jitsu tournaments? Does Brazilian jiu-jitsu have many leg locks?**

That is a good question. For a long time you didn't see a lot of leg locks because of the rules. In the tournaments in Brazil, 10 or 20 years ago, those things were not allowed. Now, though, they are legal and you see a lot more knee bars, heel hooks, and foot locks. The heel hook, though, which puts so much pressure on the knee and the hip, and can cause very serious damage, is the one that jiu-jitsu schools in general, I think, don't like to see in day-to-day training. No one wants to get their ligaments torn up and their knee destroyed. A lot of people just do jiu-jitsu for fun or self-defense, so I think not letting students use that move is a way of protecting them and keeping the training safe. That's the big advantage of jiu-jitsu, after all, over other martial arts — you can train really, really hard and not get hurt. So I think that jiu-jitsu teachers want to preserve that concept.

But little-by-little you see more different types of leg locks added to the jiu-jitsu arsenal. Jiu-jitsu has four different belt levels: blue, purple, brown, and black. People at the brown and the black belt level are those that have started to use more leg techniques. And that is spreading to the lower belts now.

I believe jiu-jitsu grows a little every day. The real purpose of grappling, in the Brazilian jiu-jitsu way, is to be able to apply the moves in a real situation. So you have to use moves that can cause damage. But you don't have to damage other students to practice them. So even non-leg-lock moves, such as neck cranks, are not things that I like to see students use on each other. If I see someone doing excessively dangerous moves to other students then I will tell them to stop. If they continue, then I will ask them to leave the school before anyone gets hurt.

**What is your overall philosophy of training?**

You can train a martial art, or a martial sport, such as jiu-jitsu, which is both, for sportive uses. But while you're doing this you always have to think about reality. You have to train the sportive methods, but then always keep adapting them and yourself to be able to use them in real situations. You can't lose sight of that or you lose sight of jiu-jitsu itself. That is the base idea of Brazilian jiu-jitsu — practice for sport, but be able to apply it for real.

# Chapter
## Two
# Arm
# Locks

Brazilian Jiu-Jitsu contains so many locks that the number has never been quantified. The Machado version of the style continues to modify and incorporate other locking techniques. A practitioner of Machado Jiu-Jitsu can easily flow from one lock to another, in harmony with anything his opponent may try. Locks are perfected through constant drilling, so the practitioner applies them instinctively and flows automatically, without conscious thought.

Depicted herein is a sampling of some of the more effective locks in Brazilian Jiu-Jitsu's near-infinite arsenal.

# Arm Locks

## Bent arm lock from side position

1. The defender has side control of his opponent across the face, like forming a circle across the opponent's face

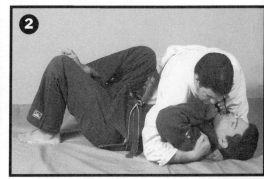

2. Defender brings his arm under the attacker's head and uses his shoulder to bring the head up, tightening the circle

3. From this position the defender has two options, he can either turn his body and grab the wrist or move his body over the opponent

4. He then pushes the arm out

5. And applies the armlock

6. Then pushes his elbow to the ground and

7. Raises the opponent's elbow to finish the lock

# Arm Locks

## This is a variation of the preceding technique, when the opponent moves the arm in the opposite direction.

1. From the same position, the opponent moves his arm up

2. The defender crosses over the opponent's body and

3. Moves so he is facing his opponent's feet

4. He sits backward

5. Pinning the opponent, and

6. Applies an arm-bar

# The same technique from the reverse angle

1. From the same position, the opponent
moves his arm up

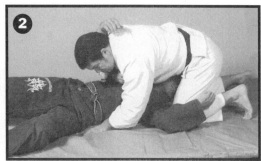

2. The defender crosses over
the opponent's body and

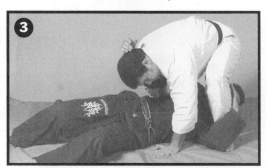

3. Moves so he is facing his opponent's feet

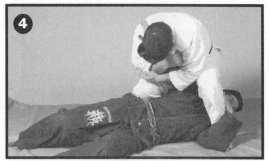

4. He sits backward

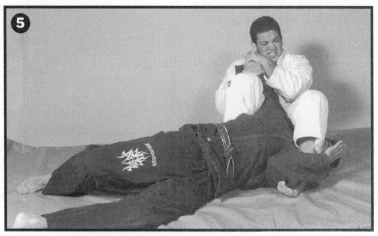

5. Pinning the opponent and applies an arm-bar

## Arm bar when opponent is on all fours

1. Defender has applied mount

2. Defender places his knee on opponent's head

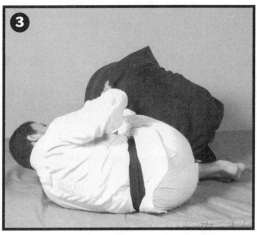

3. Defender lies down on his side, bringing
opponent's body around with him

4. He reaches up and grabs the opponent's leg

5. And applies the arm bar

# Side control to bent arm lock

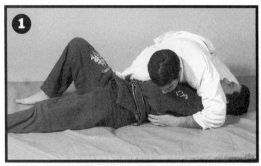

1. From the side position, the defender controls the attacker's wrist

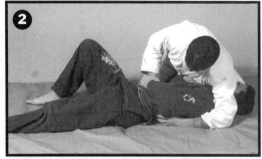

2. Then raises the elbow up to

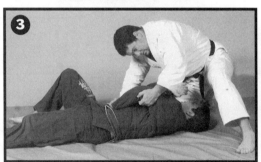

3. Take control of the arm in a Figure-4. It is very important to keep the leg up to force the opponent to turn his body

4.This turns the opponent over on his back

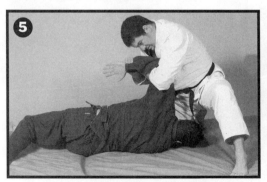

(5 & 6) Which allows the defender to finish the technique, called a "Kimura"

## Arm bar from the side mount

*1. From the side position*

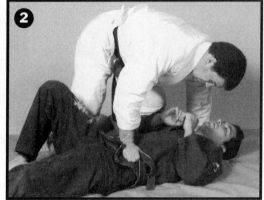

*2. The defender grabs the belt*

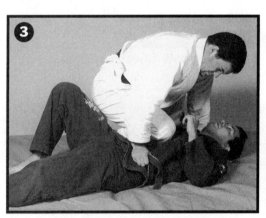

*3. Over 70% of the time, the reaction is to push the knee out*

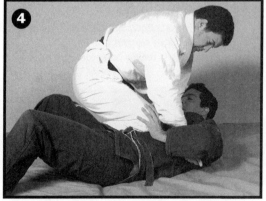

*4. Which is immediately countered by an arm-bar*

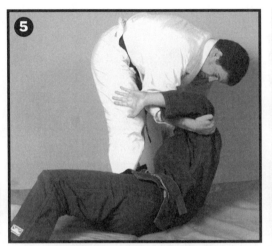

5. The defender stands and raises the
opponent's body from the ground

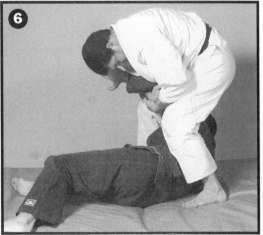

6. Turns around

7. And drops back into an arm-bar

# Arm Locks

**A variation of the previous technique. Instead of doing an arm-bar, this technique ends in an "elbow crank."**

1. From the side position

2. The defender grabs the belt and rises

3. However, when the opponent pushes

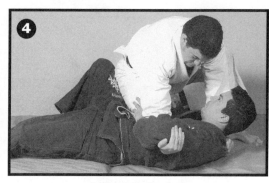
4. The defender rises

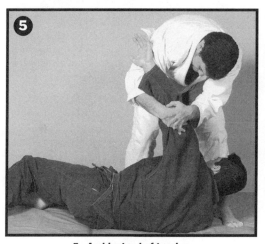
5. And instead of turning

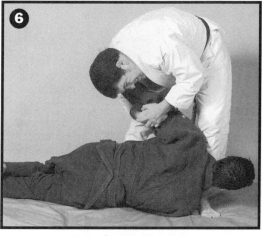
6. Applies the arm crank

# The same technique from a different angle

1. From the side position

2. The defender grabs the belt and rises

3. However, when the opponent pushes

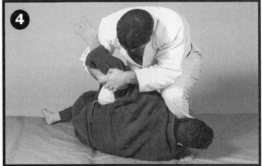

4. The defender rises

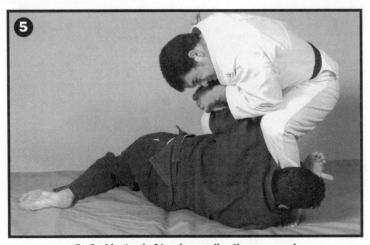

5. And instead of turning applies the arm crank

# Arm Locks

## Bent arm lock from the bottom

*1. The defender is on the ground*

*2. He turns his body to the right*

*3. And grabs the attacker's arm*

*4. He controls the arm as he turns*

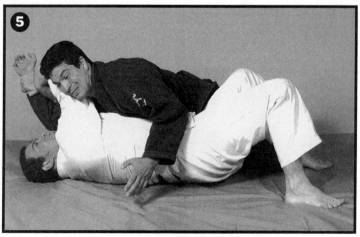

*5. In the other direction*

# Arm lock from the bottom position

1. The defender is on the ground

2. He pops his hip up

3. And turns his body to the side

4. Then brings his legs up

5. And applies a lock to the arm

# Arm Locks

## Double arm control

1. The attacker has the defender on the ground, but the defender has his feet up

2. He takes control of the arm of the attacker

3. And brings his legs around

4. Locking a triangle

5. With both hands on his shoulder

6. He pulls the shoulder down, creating leverage on the elbow

# Arm bar variation of previous technique

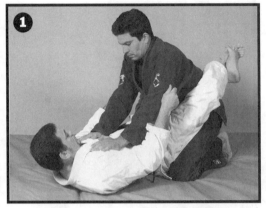

*1. Again the attacker has the defender down*

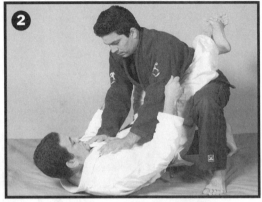

*2. With both hands, he controls the arm*

*3. Brings the elbow close to him*

*4. And moves his hip outward*

*5. This causes the opponent to come down, and the defender can wrap his leg, cranking the arm*

# Arm Locks

## Arm bar when opponent stands up

1. The attacker has the defender down

2. The attacker attempts to stand

3. As he attempts this the defender locks
his legs around the attacker's back

4. Restraining him

5. By taking hold of his elbows

6. He then begins to turn

7. And releases the elbows and swtiches his arm position to control the wrist

8. And spins around to apply the lock

# Arm Locks

## Simple armlock from the guard

1. The attacker has the defender down

2. The defender brings both of his hands between the opponent's arms and pushes the arms out

3. When the arms are open, the defender switches his arm position and grabs the attacker's wrists

4. He then sits up

*5. And grabs his own wrist*

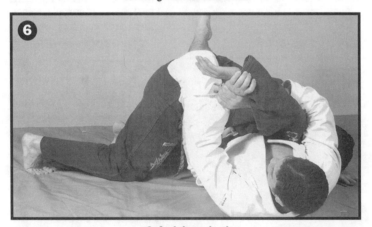

*6. And drops back*

*7. Into the finish*

## Bent arm lock with the leg

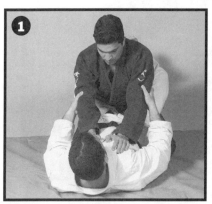

*1. The attacker has the defender down*

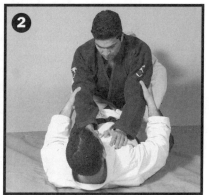

*2. As in the previous technique, the defender brings his arms together inside the attacker's arms, pushing them out*

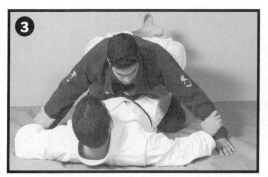

*3. He puts his knee inside the attacker's arm*

*4. Then turns to his left*

*5. Swings his leg over the attacker's arm to trap it*

*6. Sits up and leans into the finishing position*

# Arm lock from the mount position

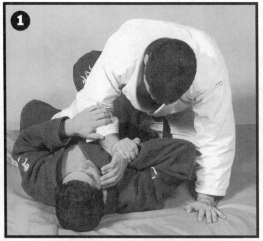

1. Defender has opponent on the ground and control over the right wrist

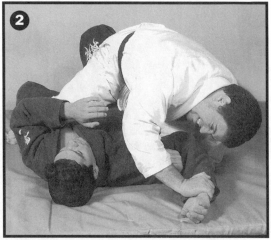

2. He moves to his left, pressing the arm to the floor

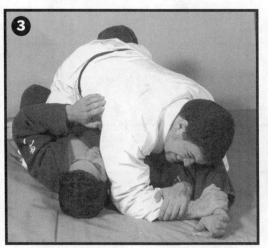

3. He then slips his left arm under the opponent's arm and grabs his own forearm to lock

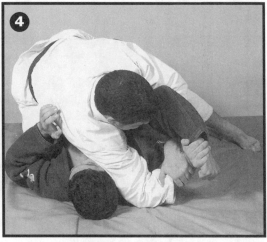

4. He shifts his weight sideways to crank the arm

# Arm Locks

## Arm bar from the back

*1. Defender locks his hands together under the opponent's arm*

*2. He stands and places his left leg over the defender's body*

*3. He then places his other leg in front of the attacker's face*

*4. He then sits down*

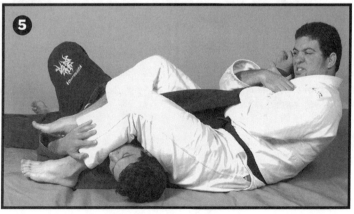

*5. And cranks back on the arm*

# Arm lock from standing position

1. Defender fakes a throw

2. Then grabs the arm

3. Moves his body around and downward to control the opponent

4. Uses his leg to trap the opponent

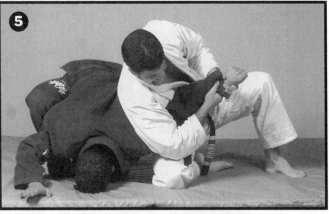

5. And drops back to apply the lock

# Arm Locks

## Flying arm bar from standing position

1. The opponents are in a standing position

2. The opponent begins to attempt a throw by pulling back

3. And placing his foot on the defender's stomach

4. The defender pulls the attacker into him

*5. Grabs his sleeve and jacket*

*6. Then twists his body*

*7. Taking him down*

# Chapter Three

## Leg Locks

Machado Jiu-Jitsu, unlike several other forms of Brazilian Jiu-Jitsu, contains a vast array of leg locks. The leg locks were refined over the years by the Machado brothers and added to the system as the style evolved. Leg locks are enormously effective moves in the ring and in the street. When practicing these techniques, the student is reminded to use minimal pressure and release the pressure the instant the opponent taps. The reason for this is that the legs are very long and, as a result, the "leverage" effect is very powerful, and even a small amount of pressure can cause a great deal of pain.

# Leg Locks

## "Banana split"

*1. The defender grabs the opponent's belt*

*2. He presses down and turns to the side*

*3. Then grabs the opponent's right foot*

*4. He places his other foot behind the opponent's ankle*

*5. Pulls back on the leg while lying back*

*6. And cranks on the leg*

# When the opponent is on all fours

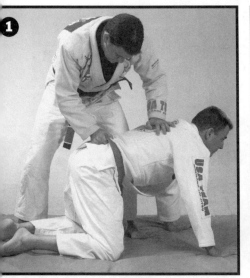

1. The defender has his opponent down on all fours

2. He wraps one arm around the opponent's torso and presses down with his body

3. Then grabs the opponent's foot

4. And lays down on his body while pulling back on the foot

# Leg Locks

## Leg bar from outside in

1. The defender has his attacker on his back. He grips the opponent's leg

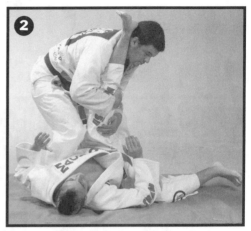

2. He then stands up

3. And kneels down on the opponent's inner thigh

4. The defender then lies back

5. And applies the leg bar

# Same as previous technique from inside out

1. The defender has control
of the opponent's leg

2. He stands up

3. He wraps his leg
around the leg his
is controlling

4. And lies back,
cranking the leg

# Leg Locks

## Straight foot lock

1. The opponent is on his back. The defender presses the knees open

2. He then wraps the left leg

3. Pulls up

4. And applies the lock

## Same as previous technique finished on ground

*This technique is the same as the previous technique (1 & 2) but instead the defender lies down to the side and applies the lock (3 & 4)*

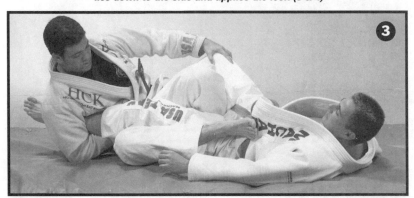

# Leg Locks

## Heel hook finish

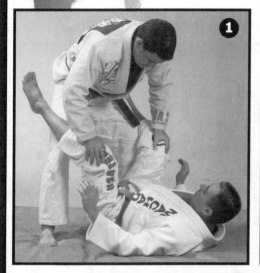

*This technique begins as the previous two techniques (1 & 2); however, the defender lies down on his side and finishes with a heel hook (3-7, next page)*

# Leg Locks

## Footlock from side position

1. The defender has his attacker pinned, lying across his body

2. He reaches under the opponent's leg

3. Stands up slightly

4. And locks his hands over the ankle, cranking the opponent

## Footlock from standing position

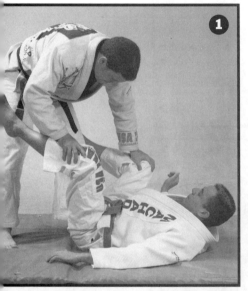

*Beginning in the same position as the previous technique (1 & 2) the defender then crosses the opponent's leg over his knee (3) and applies a footlock (4)*

# Leg Locks

## Cross leg lock

1. The opponent has his attacker on his back. He presses down on the attacker's knee

2. He wraps his arm under the attacker's left leg

3. And stands up

**4. Then locks his hands to secure the leg**

**5. And lies back**

**6. And wraps his leg around the opponent's left leg, completing the lock**

# Leg Locks

## Leg lock from half guard

1. The defender has his opponent in the half guard

2. He presses his arm against the throat while shifting to the side

3. While pressing the opponent down, he stands up and pulls back on the leg

4. He leans forward, wrapping his arm further around the leg

5. And sits back to apply the lock

# Leg lock counter against attempt to hook leg

The defender's opponent attempts to hook his leg

2. The defender places his left leg in back of the opponent's leg

3. Turns around completely while grabbing the leg

4. And drops back to apply the lock

# Leg Locks

## Leg lock from inverted position

1. The defender had his opponent pinned in the inverted position

2. He wraps his arm around the leg

3. And sits up while pressing down on the opponent's body

*4. He sits back*

*5. Cranking on the leg*

*6. And drops
onto his back*

*7. Locking the leg*

## Different set-up for footlock from guard

*1. Defender has his opponent on the ground*

*2. The opponent scissors him and the defender falls forward on his hands*

*3. He leans forward*

**4. Then twists his body**

**5. And grabs the opponent's foot to apply the lock**

# Leg Locks

## Set up for counter for escape from mount position (footlock)

1. The attacker has the defender pinned

2. The attacker arches his back and reaches up to the opponent's chest

3. Then jacknifes his legs forward

4. Pushing on the attacker

5. He then shifts his weight and turns his body to the side

6. Completing a reversal

7. And applies the lock

# Leg Locks

## Set up for heel hook mount position

*1. The attacker has the defender on his back*

*2. The defender pushes at the belt line while raising one knee*

*3. To push the attacker to the side*

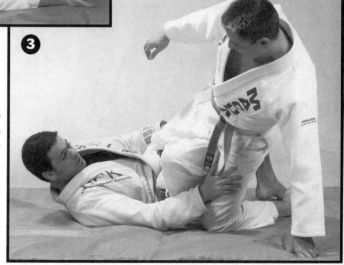

**4. As the attacker goes down to the side**

**5. The defender applies the heel hook and locks the leg**

# Leg Locks

## Advanced set-up for leg lock from guard

1. The attacker and defender are on the ground. The defender grabs the attacker's lapel

2. He turns around and begins to stand

3. Leaning forward

4. He reaches down and hooks up with his leg under the armpit

5. And begins to roll

6. This motion turns the oponent over

7. To where the defender can apply an armlock

# Leg Locks

## Set up for heel hook from guard position

*1. The attacker has the defender down. The defender pulls on the attacker's arms while reaching up with his feet*

*2. He hooks his leg around the back of the attacker's leg*

*3. He then hooks his other leg around the attacker's midsection*

*4. He brings the attacker down*

*5. And locks his arms around the ankle*

# Leg Locks

## Leg lock from open guard position

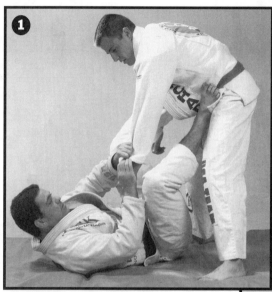

1. The defender is on the ground with control of his opponent's wrist. He presses one foot up into the attacker's midsection

2. From this position, he wraps his arm around the opponent's ankle

3. And hooks his leg around the opponent's leg

**4. He then twists his body and pulls the opponent down**

**5. And locks the leg**

# Leg Locks

## Takedown with footlock combination

1. The attacker and defender face each other, each gripping the other's gi

2. The defender leans forward against the attacker's arm

3. And grabs the attacker's leg

4. He lifts the leg

5. And turns his body

6. Taking the attacker down

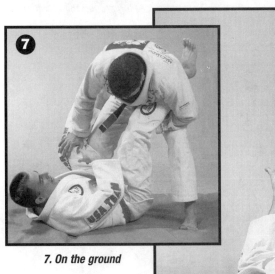

7. On the ground

8. He completes the lock

# Leg Locks

## Scissor takedown with combination leglock

1. The opponents grappling, the defender grabbing the attacker's wrist

2. He wraps his leg around the attacker

3. And pushes off the ground to scissor his opponent

4. This takes him down

5. To where the defender can apply a leg lock

# Leg Locks

## Set up standing position/leg bar

1. The defender grabs the attacker's sleeve

2. He turns, putting his leg between the attacker's legs

3 .Then leans forward

4. To grab the opponent's foot

5. He then reaches up with his other leg

6. Wraps the attacker from the back

7. And takes him down in a lock

# Chapter Four

## Chokes

Chokes are one of the ultimate weapons in the Brazilian Jiu-Jitsu arsenal. The student is reminded to use minimal force in that they are very dangerous. Many chokes cut off oxygen to the brain and full pressure should never be applied during practice.

The Machado system of Brazilian Jiu-Jitsu contains a vast array of chokes. It is important not to know simply how to apply the choke, but how to deliver it (in other words: get yourself into a position to apply the choke). Chokes are usually considered the "coup de grace" (end) of a fighting move. Entire techniques are depicted to show the student effective entries.

# Chokes

## Simple choke

1. The attacker has the defender on his back. The defender reaches up to the side of the neck

2. He then crosses the opponent's neck by grabbing the lapel

3. He pulls his opponent forward in a choke

## Same choke from another angle

*1. The defender reaches up and grabs the collar*

*2. He pulls the attacker down to the side while reaching around with his other hand*

*3. And crosses his hands, applying the choke*

# Chokes

## Side Choke

1. From cross position the defender opens collar

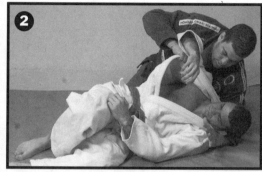

2. Feeds collar to hand

3. Traps arm and puts hands behind head

4. To create guillotine leverage

5. Choke complete

# Reverse choke from cross-face

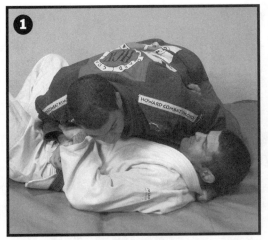

*1. The defender has his opponent pinned from the side*

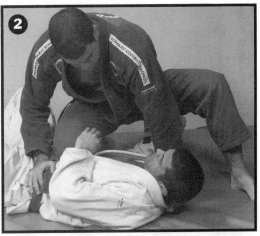

*2. He presses down on the opponent's beltline*

*3. Applies a choke across the face*

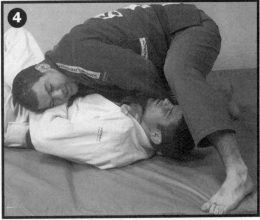

*4. And spins leg all the way around to finish choke*

# Chokes

## "Killing the lion"  (back choke)

1. The defender has the attacker on the ground

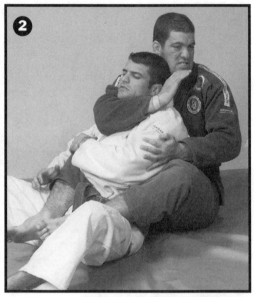

2. He wraps his arm around the neck

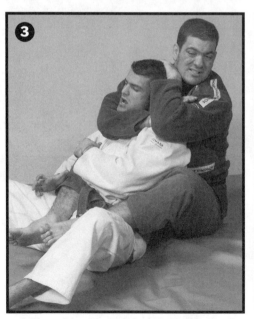

3. Then places his other hand behind the head

4. And applies pressure

# Collar back choke

1. From the back defender opens collar

2. Reaches around the top

3. While wrapping his other arm under
the body

4. And feeds collar pressure down and up
creating the choke

# Chokes

## Front spinning choke

*1. From the front*

*2. The defender puts his arm around his opponent's neck*

*3. And lies down on his side*

*4. Bringing his opponent's lapel up to choke him*

# Variation of collar choke

*Same as previous technique (1 & 2); however, instead of grabbing the collar the hand comes behind the head (3 & 4).*

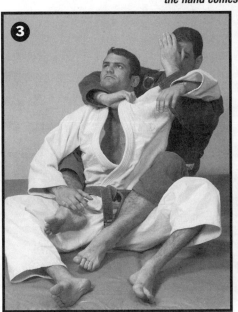

# Chokes

## Penetrate hooks, flatten the body and neck depression

*1. From the back*

*2. The defender puls his arms under the attacker's arms*

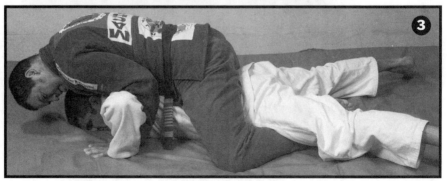

*3. And hooks the legs, pushing backward and forward simultaneously to flatten the opponent*

**4. He wraps his
arm around the
opponent's neck**

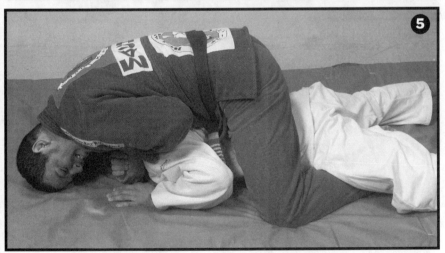

**5. And lies for-
ward, applying
the choke**

# Chokes

## Variation of previous, but going for "clock" position

1. As in the previous technique, the defender has his opponent down

2. He again pulls his arms under the opponent's arms

3. However, this time he steps out with his right foot, then brings his left foot around as well

4. This rotates his entire body like the hands of a clock

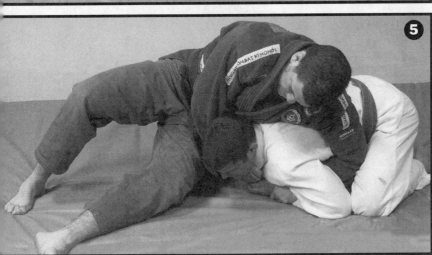

5. As he pushes the opponent down

# Chokes

## Simple choke from mount position

1. The attacker is on his back

2. The defender reaches around to the side of the neck

3. Then grabs the attacker's lapel

4. And leans forward

5. To finish technique

# Simple choke from mount position (palm down grip)

*1. The defender has the attacker down*

*2. He locks arms around his head*

*3. Grabs his own sleeve*

*4. Goes around the neck*

*5. And leans forward*

# Chokes

## Simple triangle

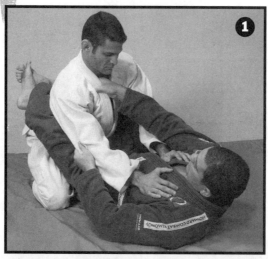

**1. Defender opens his guard**

**2. Pressing outward on the opponent's arm**

**3. Then brings his right leg up**

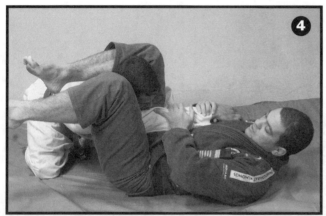

4. And down to

5. Trap the head

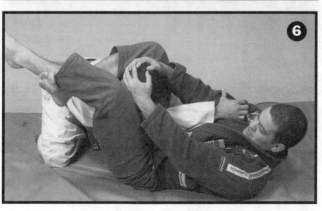

6. And locks the triangle

# Chokes

## Same technique but from the open guard position

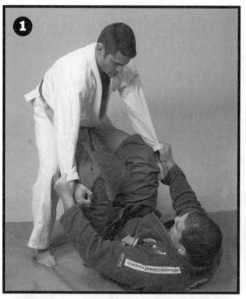

*1. In this variation the attacker is standing*

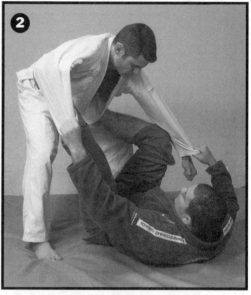

*2. He pulls on the attacker's sleeves*

*3. Hooks a leg around his neck*

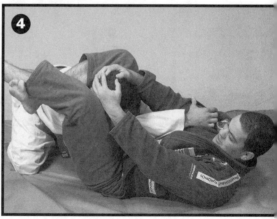

*4. And pulls him down into the choke*

## Set-up for the front choke

*1. Defender traps the collar*

*2. Steps to the side*

*3 And reaches up to apply the choke*

# Chokes

## Triangle from the back

1. The defender has his attacker on the ground

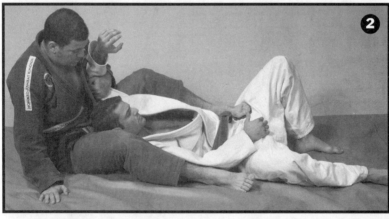

2. He grabs his arm and hooks his foot around, pressing on the attacker's thigh

3. He hooks his other foot around the attacker's body

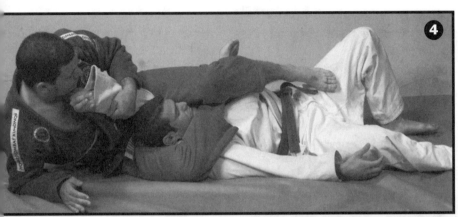

**4. Locking the foot under his other leg**

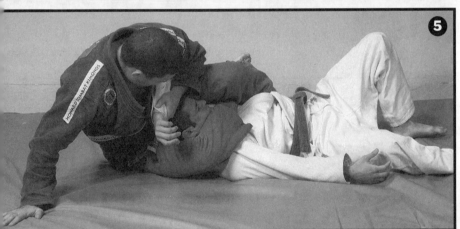

**5. And leans into the attacker**

**6. Applying the choke**

# Chokes

## Crucifix

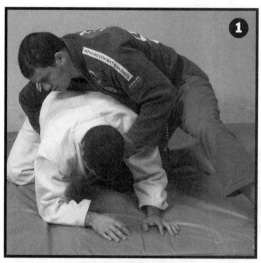

1. The defender is on his attacker's back from the side

2. He wraps his hands while stepping back

3. Drops forward

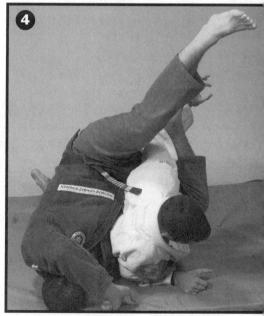

4. Rolls over while keeping his arm wrapped around the opponent

**5.** Pulling the opponent over

**6.** To where the defender can reach up to the side of the neck, fingers extending

**7.** And place his other arm under the attacker's arm, completing the choke.

# Chapter Five

## Without the Gi

As explained earlier in this book, the world of grappling is rapidly changing. Due to the advent of various "no-holds-barred" events and other forms of competition, many students want to train without the gi. The gi has become the uniform of traditional grappling arts, even though it is derived from the Japanese clothing of the era in which judo was developed (late 1800's – early 1900's). As a result, many techniques include the assumption that the opponent will be wearing a gi, and there are techniques which actually seek to turn the opponent's gi into a weapon to use against him.

Therefore, this section on training without the gi has been included. Although the vast majority of Brazilian Jiu-Jitsu techniques are universal, and work with or without the gi, this section deals specifically with "non-gi" techniques. These are especially applicable in "non-gi" competitions and street situations.

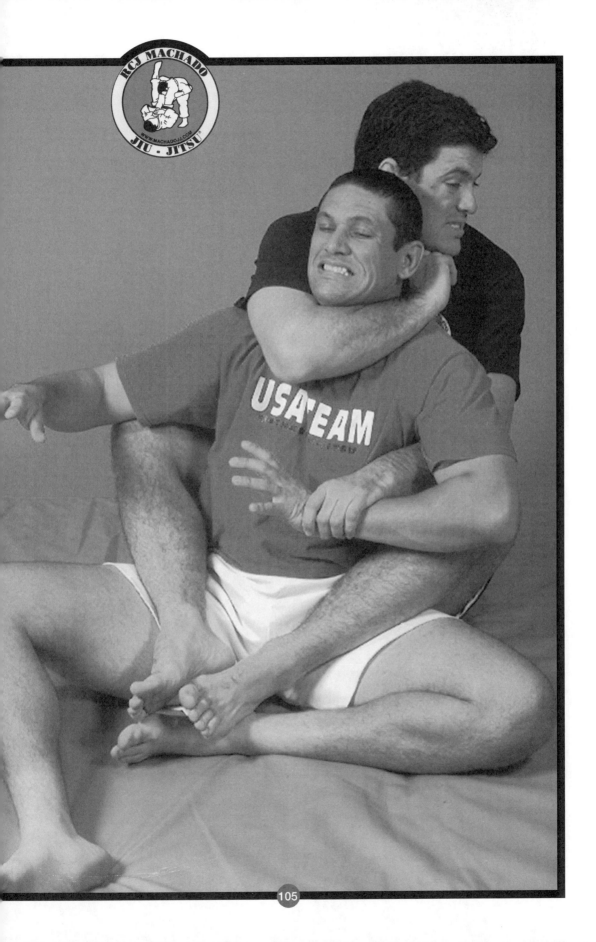

## Basic armlock

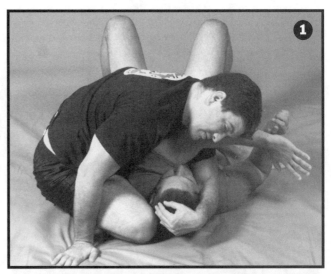

1. Defender has his opponent down, his arm wrapped through and under one of his opponent's arms

2. Defender presses down on the ground for leverage and lifts on the trapped arm

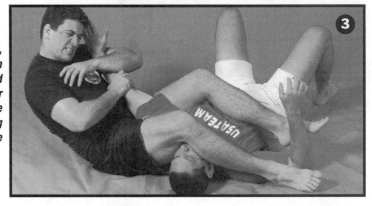

3. He lies back, pulling the arm between his legs and placing his legs over the opponent's face and body, creating tremendous leverage

# Arm crank

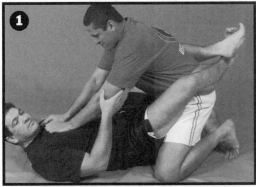

1. The opponent has the defender on his back

2. The defender wraps his legs around opponent's torso and brings his arms up between the opponent's arms to break the hold

3. He grabs the opponent's wrist

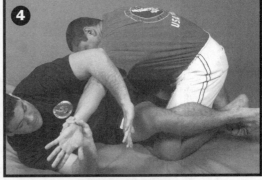

4. Then wraps his other arm around the opponent's arm

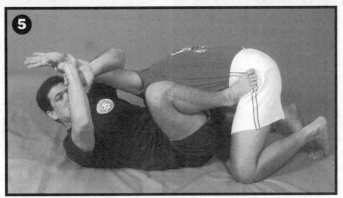

5. He then pulls the arm back into the lock and presses on the opponent's thighs to create pressure.

## Arm crank

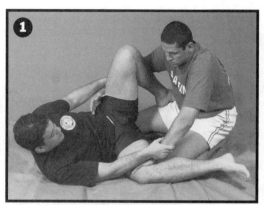

1. Opponent has the defender down

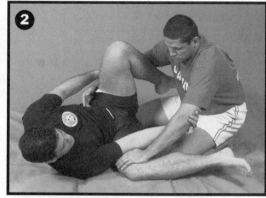

2. Defender reaches around the arm and grabs the elbow from the outside

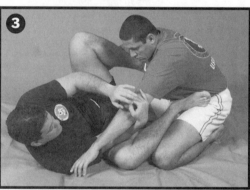

3. Then presses back on the opponent's torso with his foot and grabs the elbow with his other hand

4. He pushes back with his foot

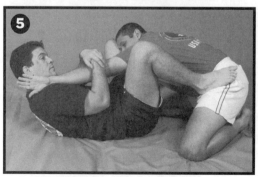

5. Shifts his position onto his back while pulling down on the outside of the elbow

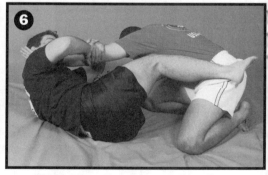

6. And puts on the pressure, locking the arm

# Arm lock from the guard

1. The defender, on his back, grabs his attacker's wrists

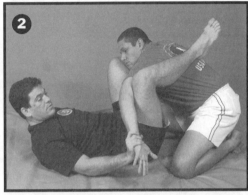

2. He brings his legs up around the opponent's body

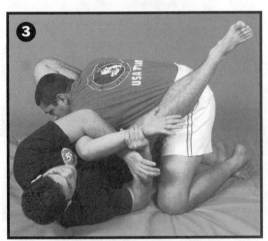

3. While wrapping his arm through the inside of the opponent's arm

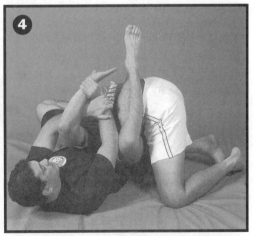

4. He then presses down with his legs and pulls back on the arm

## Arm lock from the guard

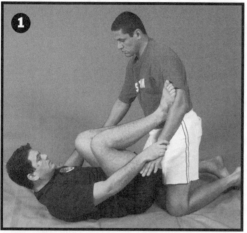

1. The defender, on his back, grabs the opponent's wrists and presses on his arm with his right foot

2. Then grabs the other arm and brings his leg around the opponent's neck

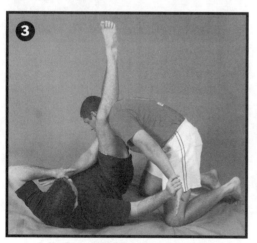

3. He then shifts his body on the ground

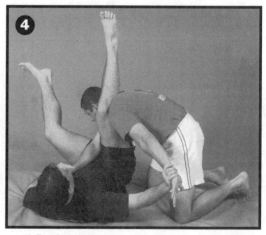

4. Forcing the opponent to the opponent's right

5. He then scissors the arm

6. To complete the lock

## Simple choke from behind

*1. The defender has the best of the attacker*

*2. He now must finish the confrontation, so he wraps one arm around the attacker's neck*

*3. In a "V," compressing the carotid arteries*

*4. Then brings his other arm up*

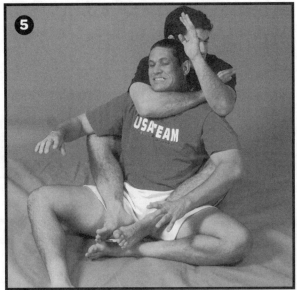

5. To wrap
the neck
from the
other side

6. Completing
the choke

## Triangle

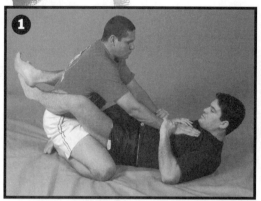

1. The defender is on his back

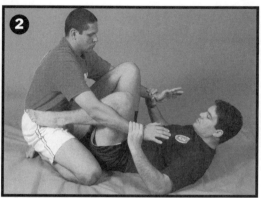

2. He grabs his opponent's wrists and presses on the opponent's torso with his feet

3. He then reaches up with his feet, the right leg inside the arms, the left leg outside

4. And wraps the right leg around the neck

5. He then brings up the left leg and locks the right foot under it

6. To apply the choke

# Guillotine from the ground

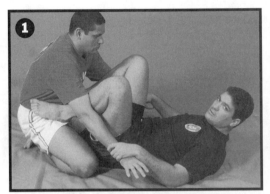

1. The attacker has the defender on his back

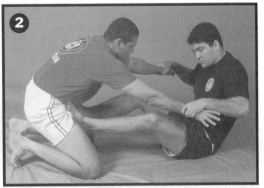

2. The defender pulls on the attacker's wrists and presses on his midsection

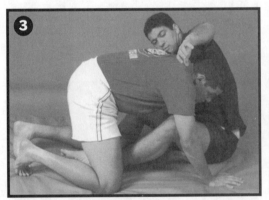

3. He then quickly reaches over the attacker's head with his left hand

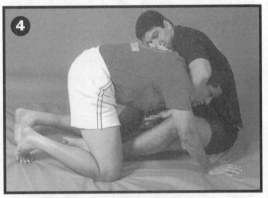

4. Wraps his arms around the opponent's neck

5. And bends the neck downward, creating pressure

6. He then wraps his right leg around the opponent as he applies the choke

## Neck crank from open guard position

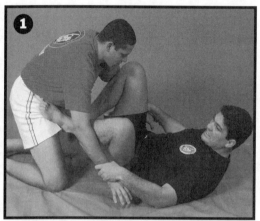

1. The opponent has the defender on his back, and the defender grabs his wrists and presses on his body with his feet

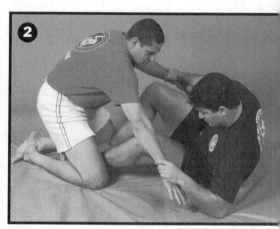

2. He then sits up,

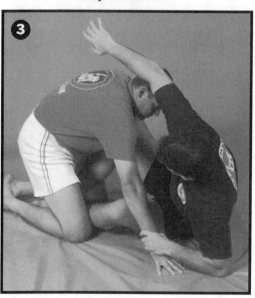

3. pulling on the opponent to help him rise

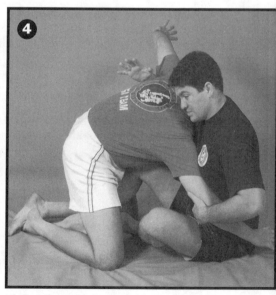

4. And places his head next to the opponent while wrapping his arm around and under the opponent's arm

5. He then twists
his body, taking
the opponent down

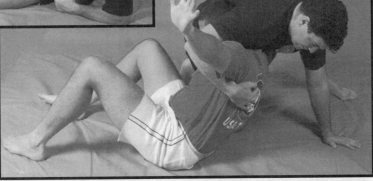

6. Presses his hand
on the ground to
create leverage

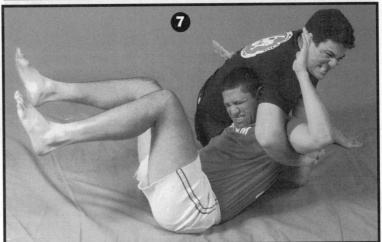

7. And cranks
upward, creating
a choke

## Ground choke from the back

1. The defender grabs his opponent's shoulder

2. He brings the opponent's head down

3. Then spins around and gets on the opponent's back

4. Where he reaches under the opponent's arms

5. And pushes down with his midsection to force the opponent down

6. Now he is free to apply a choke

## "Kimura" from the side

1. The opponent is down

2. The defender shifts his position

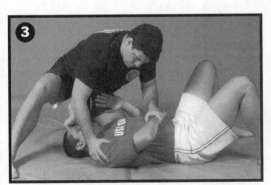

3. And presses down on the opponent's wrist

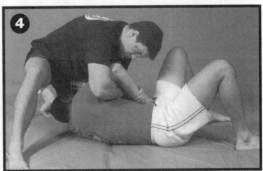

4. Then wraps his other arm through the opponent's arm

5. Applying pressure

6. And cranking the arm

## Bent arm lock from the side position

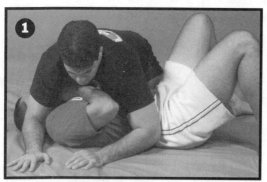

1. The defender has his opponent down

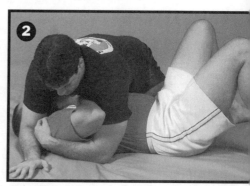

2. He reaches up and grabs the shoulder

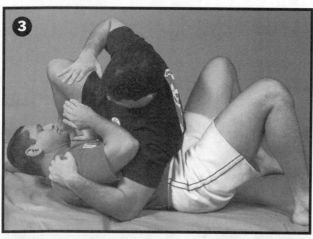

3. Then turns his body to the side

4. And grabs the wrist

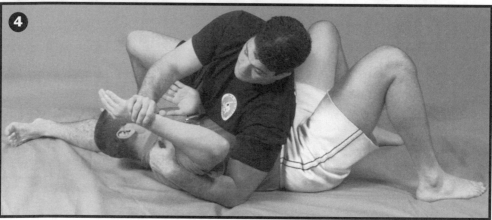

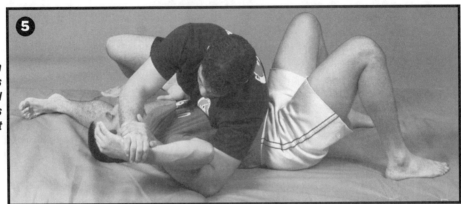

5. He then locks his hand around his wrist

6. And presses the arm to the ground

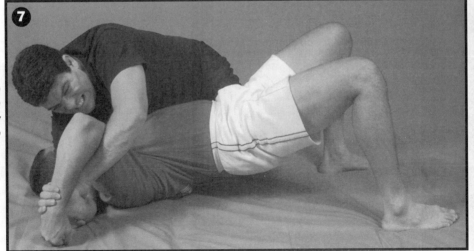

7. Where he can apply pressure

# Without the Gi

## Armlock from the side

*1. The defender has his opponent pinned*

*2. He grabs the opponent's wrist*

*3. And leans into the arm with his shoulder*

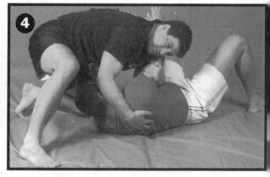

*4. He then reaches under the opponent's body*

*5. And spins around*

*6. Pulling the arm out into the lock*

# Arm lock from side control

1. The defender has his opponent down

2. He rises up, grabbing the opponent's arm

3. And presses on the outside of the arm

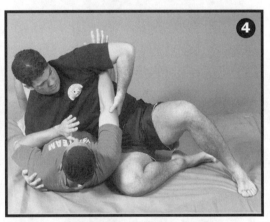

4. As he twists his body around

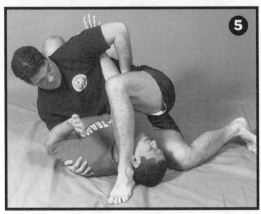

5. He then brings his left leg over the opponent's head

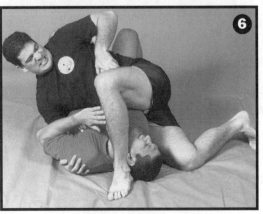

6. And cranks back on the arm

## Arm lock from the side

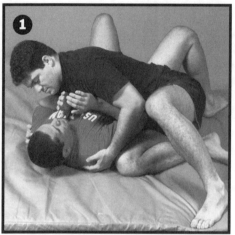

1. The defender has his attacker down

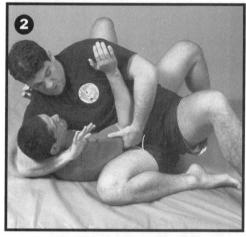

2. He stiffens his fingers and brings his hand behind the opponent's neck

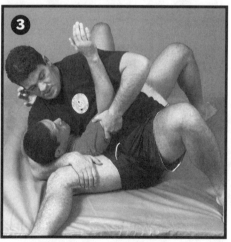

3. And applies pressure by grabbing his own leg and pulling upward on the opponent's arm

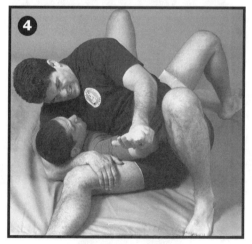

4. He leans forward

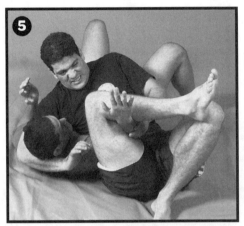

5. Then brings the opponent's hand under his leg

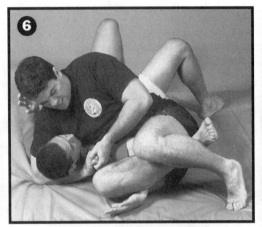

6. Trapping the arm completely

7. And applies the choke

## Leg Lock from the hooks

1. The opponent has the defender down and the defender immediately grabs the opponent's wrist and reaches up with his legs

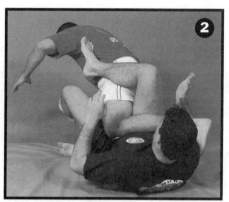

2. He brings his leg around, taking the opponent down

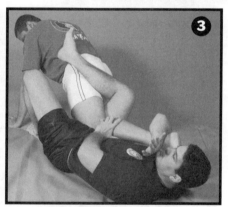

3. And grabs the opponent's leg

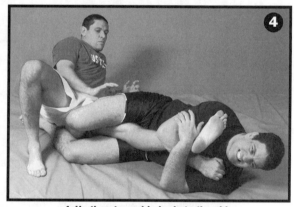

4. He then turns his body to the side

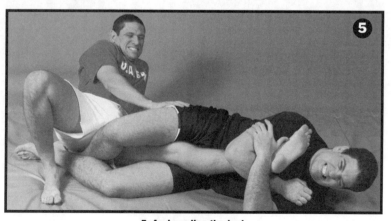

5. And applies the lock

# Heel hook

1. The defender has the attacker on his back and begins by pressing outward on the legs

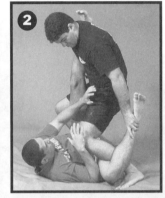

2. He then drops down with one knee to pin the arm

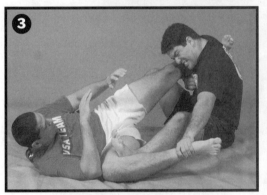

3. Then sits back

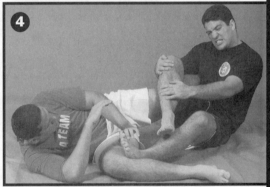

4. And wraps his leg around the outside of his opponent's leg

5. He then locks the ankle and lies back, applying the leg lock

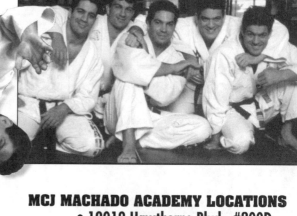